SECRETS OF MASTERING THE ART OF HOME SELLING: HOW TO USE THE 30/60/90+-DAY PRICING FORMULA… FOR YOUR MARKETPLACE!

BY
JIM A. URBAN

SECRETS OF MASTERING THE ART OF HOME SELLING: HOW TO USE THE 30/60/90+-DAY PRICING FORMULA...FOR YOUR MARKETPLACE!

Copyright © 2009 by Jim A. Urban

URBAN COMPANIES
"Your Family Realtor"
One Union Square
143 Union Blvd, Suite 110
Lakewood, Colorado 80228
Office direct (303) 933-7000 | (303) 459-6822 (fax)
toll free 1-800-25URBAN (1-800-258-7226)

ISBN: 1-442115-79-3
ISBN13: 978-1-442115-79-8

Printed in the United States of America.

Special Notes

REALTOR® is a registered trademark of the National Association of REALTORS (NAR) and is not intended to be used as a generic term. Readers must understand that not all real estate agents are affiliated with and a member of an association designating that agent as a REALTOR®. Jim A. Urban of Urban Companies is a member of the Jefferson County Association of Realtors and is a member of the National Association of Realtors. Stories or other references to other real estate agents in this book may or may not be affiliated as a REALTOR®.

Agent or Consultant? In my book when I refer to an agent, this refers to those typical real estate agents in the business today. In short, the words "traditional real estate agent" to me paint a picture of a pushy and quick deal closer. A real estate consultant, on the other hand, is someone I view as a trusted advisor, someone who puts the customer before anyone else's needs including his own! I am not trying to change how our culture refers to a real estate "agent." I am just suggesting that using "real estate consultant" paints a different picture in our mind as someone in our profession. Believe me, I know through real life experience that there is a difference. After all, the word agent sounds too much like "Secret Agent" and I don't want you to keep me a secret! I would like my clients to get used to referring to me as their consultant and I would like to dialogue with language that begins with "As your consultant..." For example, "As your consultant, I recommend we draw up a counterproposal that would put an extra $3000 in your pocket at our closing celebration, fair enough?"

In the interest of brevity, clarity and consistency, I use the generic pronouns he, him and his throughout this book.

About the author

Jim A. Urban has held his Colorado Real Estate License and worked in the field since 1984. He is a Certified Residential Specialist (CRS) and alumni member of By Referral Only. Jim attended the University of Northern Colorado and majored in Business Administration.

Married since 1982, Jim and his wife Susan have four daughters: Bethany, 24; Elissa, 22; Kendra, 19, and Janelle, 16. Their oldest, Bethany, is married to Casey Jackman.

Jim's interests include bicycling, family, vacations, travel, and leading and inspiring others. Bicycling is a great passion of his. He participates at least three times a year in organized road cycling rides like Bicycle Tour of Colorado, Ride The Rockies, The Triple By Pass and various charity rides.

Reading business and self-help books is a hobby of Jim's. He is part of a weekly book readers club that reads and discusses at least two to three books a year. The club has had success inviting authors to visit. Jim also hosts a monthly Mastermind group with like-minded professionals in the Denver area.

Jim loves to blog (www.JimsJournal.net). He posts at least twice a week and works at finding ways to help clients, family, friends, neighbors, co-workers and peers in the real estate business. He enjoys inventing new and better ways to make humans have a better life on this planet. He also is very involved in his church, the Church of Jesus Christ of Latter Day Saints, and has a passion to help and serve people. Jim's second daughter is currently serving a mission for the church in Buenos Aires, Argentina.

those you coach and train. Because of you, I went from my old ways of finding new clients to the ways that bring much more joy to this business! You are part of an amazing team and I am forever grateful you chose to be on the team. One good place to find Dean is at www.MarketingMonday.com

The list could go on and I know I am missing so many close people and that is not my intention. I will say that you know who you are if I have missed your name. If you get my monthly newsletter in the mail, you are one of those people I could have listed here!

Dedicated to . . .

This book is dedicated to Joe Stumpf, the greatest coach and mentor on the planet. Thanks for your encouragement and your example of how to think big! Without you, this formula would have never evolved. Thanks for believing in this formula and seeing its value to the world, and for being a great friend. I look forward to more innovations as you continue to inspire me and the world. You took this strategy and turned it into a "Magic Words" formula! You have taught me to always be seeking, discovering, and growing. The real estate and mortgage industry is amazingly blessed to have you as a mentor and leader as we follow your cutting edge systems for a better life.

Introduction

The idea for the 30/60/90+ Pricing Formula came to me during a two-and-a-half day strategic forum conference in the fall of 2006. It was born out of a sense of frustration – mine and my peers in the real estate business – over the struggles sellers were having in selling their homes. I remember sitting in my lovely hotel room overlooking the lush pool area thinking, *What can I do to help?* Maybe it was the break from my usual routine of phone calls and emails that gave me the time to think. I also believe the endorphins pumping through my veins helped – I was so excited and fired up from the conference. This contributed to my realization that the market wasn't as bad as the media had been leading us to believe, and there was a way sellers could sell!

Then it dawned on me. I had been working with a large bank, and they wanted only one thing. They wanted the *truth*! They wanted me to quote them a price called the "30-day sale value." Wow, wouldn't *any* seller want to know my opinion of a 30-day price? Well, sure they would!

When I created the formula, I realized that for home sellers to really understand the benefits of a 30-day price they must understand my professional opinion of a 60-day price and a 90+-day price. After all, the banks want more than one price quote too. I quickly Googled "home pricing formula or strategy" on the Internet and was very surprised to find little on the subject. No one had put pricing into a nice structure around the concept of time!

You see, for years after completing the paperwork and right before putting a home on the market, the seller usually asks, "Jim, how long do you think our house will be listed on the market before it sells?" Before I created the formula, I honestly couldn't even begin to answer that question. Now with the formula, all my research and study around price is based on the time frames of 30 days, 60 days and 90+ days. It answers those questions for the sellers and for me. It can do the same for you whether you are in the business or not. If not, you should ask your real estate consultant to provide his evaluation around this formula. If you decide to sell your home on your own, you should do as much research as you can around the price and think twice before you choose your final price. In fact, read this book before you select your price.

Chapter 1: *Did your Real Estate Agent ask you what price you wanted to sell for?*

Sometimes I don't even have to ask. I get a call and the potential client says, "Jim, we were referred to you by Jill" or "We noticed your real estate signs everywhere and we want to meet with you about putting our home on the market, and we want to list it for $300,000." When this happens, I don't flinch, even if I know for sure it's overpriced. After I meet with my client, review and study all the comparable homes, complete my research and show this research to the seller in person, then I ask the seller's opinion about price, because his opinion often changes once he sees the history of sales in his neighborhood.

Often, the agent asks the seller what he wants to sell for and then immediately agrees and puts the home on the market for that price! Most of the time real estate agents don't take the time to prepare and to do their homework. For newer agents especially, the pricing part of the consultation is intimidating and they are even fearful of it. There is a real art to pricing and listing a home and the art of the process takes practice and preparation! A real estate consultant who truly consults around pricing will spend at least 30 minutes on the topic of price, which includes reviewing comparable homes in the neighborhood. I've discovered that the best time to have this conversation is at or near the end of your initial consultation.

When real estate agents quote a price, they traditionally quote a single price or a price range. A price range makes more sense because to one buyer, a home is worth one price, and to another buyer it is worth a different price. There is still one problem with quoting just a price range. It's human nature: a seller always wants the highest price, even if it is unrealistic. For example, if I told my seller "Your home is worth somewhere between $275,000-$300,000," what price do you think the seller will pick? You guessed it – $300,000. This automatically puts the seller at a disadvantage. By pricing the home at the top of the range, the seller won't get a contract on his home in a timely manner. I can tell you even if the seller says he has time…he will be disappointed after about two weeks if he has not sold yet.

This is where the 30/60/90+ home pricing formula comes in. The formula forces you to relate price and time! This, of course, is what the seller really wants and this is what every real estate consultant wants his seller to understand!

Chapter 2: *The 30/60/90+ Pricing Formula gives you clarity right from the start!*

Note: When I refer to a 90+ price, I am referring to 90 days or more on the market (meaning it will be 90 days or who knows who long it will be on the market? Even months or even years!)

To the real estate community:

If you don't lay your honest opinion down from the start, your potential clients will accuse you later of not giving them the truth during your initial consultation. This is one of the beauties of this strategy: if they pick the 90+-day price and the house doesn't sell, you can remind them of the 30-day price you quoted right up front.

A quick story: A customer asked me to list his daughter's condo. In Denver, the condo market is even tougher than the single-family market. My seller insisted on a price that was between my 60- and 90+-day price. We stayed on the market for weeks before we finally got an offer. Sure enough, it came in at my 30-day price! My sellers rejected the offer and we continued the marketing. We got one offer at our 60-day price, but it was contingent on the buyer's Florida condo selling. Their market was even more of a buyer's market than ours!

After four months on the market, my sellers finally decided to rent the condo out. They never blamed me for it not selling because I had made it clear at the start that the price they wanted would require 90 or more days to sell. In the end, they realized they should have trusted me.

As real estate consultants, we have to remember that we are the consultants and the sellers are the decision makers – "The Boss." We can advise them to list at the 30-day price, but they may not choose that price. As professionals, we can choose not to work with them.

In this case, I always base my decision as a consultant on the sellers' motivation. In a declining market, if they choose either the 60- or 90-day+ price, by the time you get a contract offer or the seller finally decides to adjust to the 30-day price, the 30-day price will be lower than it was when you first quoted it! As time passes and the market falls, you now have to reevaluate the home to see where the new 30-day price may be. Conversely, in a rising market, the 30-day price could be higher. This is why you must date the 30/60/90+-day home pricing formula and net estimate document I developed. It always surprises sellers when they realize how long it has been since I initially quoted the 30/60/90+-day prices!

A quick note to homeowners:

This formula also works well when you as a home seller are in a "Short Sale" position. I won't go into great detail with what a "Short Sale" is other than it is a process of working with your bank while you are not able to make any more mortgage payments due to hardships, you owe more than your home is worth and your bank will approve your home with a short payoff. Hiring a real estate consultant to provide you with the 30/60/90+ home pricing formula will bring clarity both to you and to the mitigation department of your bank. This is a great point to remember because this formula was inspired by my interaction with banks in the broker pricing opinion process. For "Short Sales," this formula is a real natural if you or anyone you know is in this position!

Chapter 3: *The 30-day price: Where you should be*

"Why can't we just start at a higher price and just let someone make an offer?" I am asked "why?" all the time. Real estate agents are concerned they won't get the listing if they quote potential clients a truly honest 30-day price. I've learned that a certain percentage of people still can't understand the concept of a 30-day price and what it really is. A 30-day price is lower than a 60 or a 90+-day price. This is the price you quote with the utmost confidence that you can attract a bona fide, qualified, willing and able buyer within 30 days and close within about 30 days after that. It is at or even below "market value" for the neighborhood or area. It should not, however, be so much below market value that it's a giveaway (See chapter 6 on price gouging.)

The 30-day price can be referred to as:
- the "sweet spot" price
- a "price break"
- the "price point"

This is the price where it all starts to break loose! The flood gates open at this price for every home. Buyers take notice and think, "Wow, that's a pretty good deal!" It's the price that opens the door to success and a contract in your hands! Now you can start negotiating. Before this point – or if you were listed at a higher price – you were just another listing on the market. Now you are special, and real buyers can hardly contain their excitement! I have witnessed this excitement hundreds of times before. It is an unconscious thing. Buyers love the house regardless of whether it's a good deal! You can see it in their eyes and in their actions and how and what they say. You can't get back to your office quick enough to write up a contract. The key is for you as the consultant to stay calm and advise them to how they will buy this home. In a buyer's market, a home like this may be getting multiple offers and you may have to come in higher to get the winning bid. Sellers then get excited and you as their real estate consultant become their hero!

How do you find out or figure out where this price is? Can it be done scientifically? Or must it be done as a skilled and experienced artist?

Using 30/60/90+ formula is an art and shouldn't be confused with the appraisal. In my years of observation, the appraiser uses reams of data to figure the final appraisal price. The real estate consultant likewise uses data to formulate a price, but he also uses intangibles to arrive at a price. He can think like a buyer and put himself in the buyer's shoes because he's asked the buyer what's important to her and what she wants. Real-world experience and knowledge of human nature give Realtors the minds of artists. Data and research are necessary, but the artist way of thinking puts the price where this price point should be.

You see, I know what the competition is and I know what the sold data looks like. Most importantly, I have a good feel for what today's buyer wants. It takes time and experience to have this insight. Some real estate agents will never get it and this is what drives them out of the business or they choose to work with buyers only. When you have this confidence, you have a tool that few have. It took me about 10 years to really get it. Most can get this confidence of understanding, but few will wait or survive. It's all about your passion for the people. I'm sure other real estate consultants could get this insight quicker than I did, especially after reading this book.

Whenever the sellers I work with choose the 30-day price, good things always happen! Either we have sold quickly or we have had multiple offers and received as much as a 60-day price or even come close to the 90-day price in some instances!

By the way, sellers: pricing a home where it needs to be at the beginning doesn't mean you have to accept lower offers. Remember, you are in control! Many times, especially in a buyer's market, my sellers think people will always negotiate. That may be true, but choosing the 30-day price makes your property competitive, if not the *best* price. If buyers go away, they probably will come back and if they don't, it's because they are not ready or educated enough yet!

You will have another buyer within 30 days. So the key is picking the 30-day price the very first day you put your home on the market.

A quick story: I listed a home in a really tough declining market area, and out of 400 homes in this area, twelve were on the market. Only one home per month on average was selling. My sellers really wanted to get out and buy in a better part of town that included better resale value and a more stable subdivision. My clients learned that if they chose my 30-day price they would have to come to closing with over $10,000 out of pocket at the closing celebration. They caught the vision of my strategy and borrowed the money to sell. The next buyer who came into the area was all over this home! He had checked out a new home property nearby that was offering big discounts, but they still couldn't beat our price. He wrote us a full-price contract! Even though the sellers had to come to closing with money, they have now been in their new home for a year and have gained in equity what they brought into closing plus even more! Even in a declining market there is always somewhere in a major metropolitan city or town where the market is good or even great! It all depends on where you live and choose to buy your home!

Time- and money-saving points about choosing the 30-day price:
· Always be the one to tell the truth about the market value or always choose the real estate consultant who is quoting the market value (30-day price) to you.
· A good way to help you determine your 30-day price is to review the for-sale homes, the sold homes and the under-contract homes. Your home should be priced near the middle of the sold value and for sure the bottom of the comparable for-sale homes.
· The value of your home is based primarily on location. Other value factors are square footage and amenities, which include the condition of the property (this being the least important of the three).

7

· You and your real estate consultant need to strategize around a price based on a rising or a declining market so you don't get caught on the market too long.

· A recent appraisal most likely will not determine your home's value. For example, an appraisal for a refinance, insurance purposes, tax assessment or a new mortgage all can be far off the actual home value today. A house is worth what a buyer is willing to pay. An accurate comparative market analysis (CMA) provided by your real estate consultant will be your most accurate determination of actual value.

· Your home is worth what a buyer is willing to pay today, not what you paid for the home or what you hope the home may be worth.

· Pricing your home where it needs to be at the beginning doesn't mean you have to accept lower offers.

· By choosing the 30-day price you will have a faster sale, less inconvenience, more prospects, more agent enthusiasm, higher offers and higher net equity!

If you're a seller, don't make the mistake of not choosing the 30-day price. You must be strict with yourself! Likewise, if you're a real estate consultant, only quote sellers the price that reflects your research around time…the time it would take to sell the home in less than 30 days!

Chapter 4: *The 60-day price: negotiating room*

People love options. Don't you love it when you are looking for a particular product and you have more than one option? We all do. According to the book *YES! 50 Scientifically Proven Ways to Be Persuasive* by Noah J. Goldstein, Steve J. Martin and Robert B. Cialdini, a study regarding options determined that not enough options discouraged the buyer, and too many options confused the buyer. When workers were offered the option of two different retirement fund options, program participation was about 75 percent. When fifty-nine funds were offered, participation fell to 60 percent.

That's the beauty of this pricing formula: it offers a perfect three options. The 60-day price quote is slightly above market value. When you list a home at a price higher than market value, it will take longer to sell. When you are looking to buy, you can determine quickly what is priced right or not. You see, the market will always adjust to your home's true value.

Selecting the 60-day price doesn't mean you will get more money; it just means it may take longer to find a buyer to write an offer to purchase. More than likely you will end up selling for the 30-day price or even lower if it takes too long to sell, especially in a declining market. Of course, there's about a one in ten chance a buyer will come along and offer you a slightly higher price and you will sell for a 60-day price. This is the chance some sellers want to take. Money is sometimes more important than timing and timing is sometimes more important than money. My point is if you start at a 30-day price and you get multiple offers you many times will get close to or even equal to the 60-day price. If you don't get multiple offers there is a very good chance you would have never gotten the 60-day price if you would have started there.

So why, you may ask, do I even quote a 60-day price if I so highly recommend the 30-day price? Because people like options, and I've come to learn that you can't convince everyone of this great formula. By offering three pricing options, it's more likely the seller will avoid the 90-day or more price and we will have a better chance of selling at least within 60 days (hopefully).

There is a common belief that if a home doesn't stay on the market for at least 60 days, the real estate consultant hasn't earned his commission. Well, my thought is if the consultant sells the home quickly, he should get paid a bonus!

Here is a quick story: I often work with an attorney who handles estate liquidation cases. These cases are handled by this attorney as county appointed personal representative or conservator deed transferred home sales. I assist him in the sale of these homes on a regular basis. From the very beginning, whenever we put one of these homes on the market, he would ask me to evaluate the home, and he always selected a price that was higher than market value. He had an understanding that he would never take advantage of the system by giving these homes away or he would lose his authority to act in behalf of these families and individuals.

Once I learned this, I asked "What if we can't get one of these homes sold someday?" The estate attorney said, "Don't worry, Jim, we won't ever let any of these homes go unsold!" More than a dozen years later and through countless homes we have handled together, he was right. We have sold everything he has given me. Here's why: each home I have listed for him, we have started at least at the 60-day price and sometimes at or near the 90-day price. When it doesn't sell within a reasonable amount of time, we adjust our price and eventually we sell each home when it hits the market value.

The problem with most average homeowners is they don't have the patience for this, or they are too emotionally tied into their own home to handle price adjustments. For example, if a homeowner chooses a 60-day price, they often get discouraged within about two and a half weeks! They try to find fault, and the person they blame is their Realtor. As a seller, if you choose the 60-day price, you should have patience and know that your house will probably not sell as fast and hopefully will sell before 60 days have passed. If you choose the 60-day price, you must agree to work together for the long haul because 60 days feels like an eternity when you're being inconvenienced during the time your home is on the market. You also may have to adjust your price lower if it doesn't sell within 60 days. You might also have to price it even lower than the originally quoted 30 day price because if you are in a declining market you may be behind the actual declining home value price. Again, this is the beauty of this formula. It prepares the home seller for more time on the market if they don't choose the 30-day price. It also should help those home sellers think twice about what's important to them – time or money – and the reasons they are selling in the first place. As in the case of the attorney above, he has all the patience in the world. He is not living in the homes we sell. I will say on occasion, when a seller chooses the 60 day price, I am surprised and we do get a higher price than expected. The question you need to ask yourself is do you have the time or money to be patient to test your price at slightly higher than market value? If so you must also work with your real estate consultant if it backfires and you find yourself having to now adjust your price lower.

Chapter 5: *The 90+-day price: Most people start here*

Homes listed at the 90+-day price do one thing and one thing only: they help other homes that are priced right sell. These home sellers will always be out there to assist those homes that are priced right!

The sad truth is that <u>most</u> sellers start too high in price. I believe it is due to getting the wrong advice or no advice at all. Often, real estate agents just ask their clients, "Where do you want to price it?" and then the home is listed for whatever the seller says. The price should be based on research not only on the comparable for-sale homes, but also the under-contract homes and recently sold or closed homes, preferably in the last six months or at most the last 12 months. I recently met with a home seller and all she could base her price on was the home around the corner, which was way overpriced. This home had been on the market for months, but she insisted that because that home was priced at this higher price, certainly she was at or near that price too. If time is not taken to review all the home sales in the area, then this formula will not work because you will not be educated on the true market value.

As I was presenting this formula at a conference, one person asked me, "Why would you even offer the 90+-day price?" Again, it's all about options, and I owe it to sellers to give them my opinion of what overpriced is. If the homeowner is considering higher than the 90-day+ price, we're not on the same page, and that allows me to decide whether I want to work with this seller at all.

Early in my career, I learned that I had to ask the right questions so that I could determine the seller's real motives and ultimately if they truly in their heart wanted or needed to sell and move on with their lives. (See Chapter 9 to learn how to ask "What is important about <u>blank</u> to you?") It's critical to help sellers understand the true desires of their heart. As real estate consultants, sometimes we must accept overpriced listings. We must help sellers through the painful process of price adjustments and consultation. Sometimes sellers will begin to understand the market after two or three weeks on the market. They need living proof that their home is really not as special and unique as they thought. They also may need to get rid of their greediness, and time usually does the trick. As a real estate consultant, if you don't have the time or patience for this, and if the seller is not truly motivated to sell and won't take it off the market, refer him to a real estate consultant in your own office. On the other hand, if the seller is motivated and will make price adjustments and is willing to endure a potentially painful process, the real estate agent may choose to work with a "listing" as apposed to a true "seller."

If only some sellers could take a reality check by going through what buyers go through. A common comment I receive from buyers who easily recognizes an overpriced listing is, "Wow, what were they thinking? Who decided on this price, the Realtor or the seller? They will never sell at that price!" In the last couple of years during this extreme buyer's market, I routinely suggest that sellers tour their competition. It really has been an eye opener and a huge success.

Recently I toured seven homes with one of my home seller clients in their neighborhood. These clients had chosen to list between the 60- and the 90+-day price. Unfortunately, the market was declining and by selecting this price, they were losing money every day. There were a few houses that were clearly overpriced and some even more overpriced than we were, but there was one particular home priced significantly lower and was an even nicer home than my sellers'. They immediately recognized it and the next day we adjusted our price to near the original 30-day price I quoted them. Within a few weeks, we had a contract offer on their home. The home that influenced us to adjust our price was still on the market, and this gave the sellers motivation to not negotiate or counter the contract offer we had in our hands. My sellers signed the contract as is and we had a wonderful closing celebration. My sellers later told me I was the best Realtor they had ever worked with.

Chapter 6: *I have no respect for real estate price gouging*

As far as I am concerned, when unethical real estate agents take advantage of sellers and price their home too low (below the 30-day price), that's price gouging. Many times, they offer lower commissions to get the listing, and they smooth-talk sellers into a lower-than-market-value price, sometimes *way* lower. I have no respect for these agents. I want you to understand the difference between the 30-day price and "price gouging."

When the going gets tough, I've seen price gouging in the bank foreclosure market. Real estate agents take advantage of some asset managers and underprice a home just so they can get a quick sale with no effort on their part and pocket easy money. I believe as a real estate consultant you must work for your income. You must earn it. If you do a good job for your seller(s) and you sell their home fast at a fair market price then you have earned it! Anything else is unacceptable! I have no respect at all for "price gouging." End of story!

Chapter 7: *Show me the net. Show me the bottom line!*

I have included in the appendix the document I use for presentations. You will notice in addition to my formula I have also included a seller net estimate. Many times when you show a seller their bottom line, even based on a 30-day price, you will get a more favorable response. Many times the price is more of a shock than the bottom line. On the other hand, this reality will really freak out those sellers with a low, zero or negative net. Regardless of the news, you must show them the numbers. It is better that they learn the truth even if it means they decide not to sell now, because this is what a true consultant does as opposed to a pushy traditional salesperson. You are there to build trust so down the road by your professionalism and good ethics they will choose to work with you. Therefore, simply DO NOT leave this step out of your initial consultation. It is critical that you and the sellers get on the same page regarding the bottom line! This also includes what you will be charging them and how you will pay a cooperating Realtor.

One very important final point that needs to be made here for real estate consultants so it does not come back to haunt you is: do not figure the net based on assumed or verbally communicated pay-off loan balances. I could write an entire new chapter just about horror stories of miscalculations and assumed pay-off balances. Instruct your sellers to dig up their most recent bank statements and go online to their mortgage company's website (or websites if they have multiple mortgages or Home Equity Lines of Credit [HELOCs]). You see, most sellers love to guess what they owe against their home. They even guess with confidence. Nine out of ten times, they are wrong, often to the tens of thousands of dollars wrong! This can result in having to cut your real estate fees, even eliminate your commission or worst of all, you could end up in court and then your license is on the line. This will destroy or come close to destroying your real estate career. Just trust me on this.

Chapter 8: *Fool- proof home selling strategies*

There are obvious things you can do to increase the value of your home. What you have to decide when it comes time to sell is if you will make any changes prior to putting your home on the market. Most people I talk to would love to do improvements to their home, but it always comes down to time and money. The first thing you should consider is getting advice up front. This is what inspired me to create my "Fool-proof Home Selling Formula" which is included in the appendices at the end of this book.

There are three parts to this formula. The first part is the home owners' selection of the 30-, 60- or 90+-day price. I simply circle which option they choose after my recommendation. Depending on what they choose as to the next two parts of the fool-proof selling strategies, the pricing may change. So you might want to work from the bottom of the form up!

The next part is home staging. Boy, has this been a big evolution over the last five to ten years! When I first got into the business this concept was never discussed, at least not in this context. Now there are tons of professional home-staging companies. They spend one to two hours with you at their initial consultation with you, going from room to room making recommendations. This takes a load off your Realtor, who in many cases has to wear too many hats. I know that too often I get sidetracked with trying to play the stager's role. I don't have that kind of extra time or expertise, especially if it is to be done right. My job is to determine whether or not the seller actually needs a professional stager. Quite frankly, there are those who really need one, there are those who don't and there are some in the middle. Staging your home does not automatically bring the value up to the overpriced range where 75 percent of for-sale homes are, or that you will get a higher price. Staging is primarily the icing on the cake that helps you sell faster and possibly raise your market value slightly. I truly am a believer in this concept, and if your Realtor recommends staging, you really should try it. By the way, there are some homes out there that need so much work it's hard to know where to begin and end with home staging. So in this case, it is better to sell the home in as-is condition.

The next area the "fool-proof home selling strategy" covers is your real estate consultant's recommendations whether to have specialists further evaluate the five major components of your home. They include:

1.) The structure
2.) The roof
3.) The heating and cooling systems
4.) The electrical systems
5.) The plumbing

Hiring a home inspector is unnecessary at this point. Many real estate agents recommend a pre-home inspection. A home inspector is a generalist. He knows a little about a lot of things. Why spend the money when in the end you will have to hire a specialist anyway? Besides, the buyer will hire his own inspector anyway regardless of whether you had your own home inspection done or not. Hiring a specialist for any one component you have concerns about makes more sense.

As an experienced real estate consultant, I can help the sellers decide which area or combination of areas needs further evaluation by a specialist before we list the home for sale. Here in Colorado an item that is often in question is the furnace. When you hire a licensed heating contractor to *clean, service, AND certify* a furnace, you now have more than likely saved yourself time, because 90 percent of the time, the inspector hired by the buyers will request that you have this work done anyway, especially on the older furnaces.

Once recommendations are made regarding the five components, I will suggest any obvious changes to the home that would significantly increase the value for little cost. There are times where some homeowners choose wrong colors, or there are simple improvements needed, and the sellers just need someone like me to tell them the truth. I use a form called the "Room by Room" review to help sellers through this process. It's less than what a staging company would do but does offer more than the average suggestions that anyone else would give.

One of my clients had some overgrown evergreen fitzer bushes in their front yard. My seller asked me if they should be removed, and I said, "Absolutely!" Within a couple of days, the bushes were gone and the house looked ten times better. Some of the neighbors asked me, "How did you get them to remove those bushes? We've been trying to get them to do that for years!" A reputable consultant has lots of influence! Even without them asking me, I would have suggested they remove these bushes, and they would have been listed as an item to do on my room by room review.

As an experienced consultant, I can tell sellers if they should have a five-year roofing certification by asking questions and eyeballing the roof from ground level. I can also recommend a professional structural engineer if I think the buyer's home inspector will have concerns. If there are any electrical or plumbing issues, it is a good idea to get one of these specialists out ahead of time to evaluate and conduct repairs.

As a result of repairs or improvements, my 30-day price can be adjusted accordingly. That's the beauty of this document I present: it puts everything into perspective and doesn't leave anyone guessing what I, their consultant, am suggesting they do or not do prior to going on the market.

Having said all of this, if the seller still doesn't want to do anything to update, fix or certify anything, I am going to say point blank it doesn't matter! What do you mean it doesn't matter, Jim? I mean price is a CURE ALL. That's right, price can cure anything. Let me explain. If the seller doesn't want to do anything to the home, you just determine the 30-day price based on the current condition of the home. I do that all the time when I complete broker price opinions (BPOs) for bank-owned properties. Most of the time the bank will do little or nothing to the property to prepare it before it hits the market for sale. The same is true with homeowners. If they refuse to do anything, that is their choice, but let them know that you are quoting a pricing formula that is determined based on its current condition. It is a CURE ALL price! It can cure the blue carpet. It can cure the pink bedroom. It can even cure the odors, a dead lawn and structural issues. You see, the right price can overcome any objection. You have to hit the right price point based on what condition the home will be in at the exact time you first put it on the market.

Chapter 9: *Hire a real estate consultant*

Before I even present the 30/60/90+ day home pricing formula to the seller, I take about 15 minutes to show them how I work, what makes me different, and hiring a consultant versus a pushy salesperson. A true consultant lays out all the options, gives his best advice and then lets the client choose. On the other hand, a salesperson has one thing in mind: a sale. Of course, this is also how real estate consultants make their living: by selling homes. I have also learned that people truly can tell if you have their best interest at heart. So my purpose is to build a relationship of trust and friendship. My goal is for my client to say as they are introducing me to others, "This is Jim Urban… he is a friend of mine in the real estate business; he will take care of you too!"

I give my potential clients four options when I first sit down to discuss their plans. "After meeting with me today you may decide…"

Your first option is…
    1.) To do nothing. (Not sell and/or buy a home.)
Your next option is…
    2.) To buy and/or sell on your own. (Without the help of a real estate consultant.)
Your next option is…
    3.) To hire a "traditional salesperson." (I ask them to define this, and I usually hear, "pushy, commission hungry, want to close the deal now!")
Or you can…
    4.) Hire a "real estate consultant." (I ask them to define this, and I usually hear, "someone who is looking out for my best interest first or my advisor").

After I give the entire presentation of the 30/60/90+-day home pricing formula, I point out that the four options are "1, 2, 3 or me, because I believe that I am the best option for you." From then on, they know the secret code for each number!

Now, if the sellers are not a 5-star client or I determine they are not ready, I may recommend option 1, 2 or even 3! You see, a true consultant gives the right advice. How do I know what advice to give? Your experience and asking the right questions is a key factor in consulting. Asking the right questions is critical because even if sellers have little equity, no equity or even if they are upside-down doesn't mean they can't move forward.

The second way to help give the right advice is to use a counseling method called the 5-6 and 7 method by my mentor Joe Stumpf. You ask your potential clients, "What is important about <u>blank</u> to you?" You fill in the blank with what they are trying to accomplish. Then you draw seven boxes on a piece of paper and you ask them questions about what is important about <u>selling your home</u> to you (or use my prepared form: see appendices)? Each question is then asked that reflects the previous answer that was given, and you fill in the answers in ascending order. Then this leads to another answer, which eventually leads to the pinnacle reasons they want to sell or buy a home, or whatever it may be. The final three answers at the top of the page, which are answers five, six and seven (5-6-7), is what needs to be focused on during the entire transaction. (See Appendix E for a copy of the form I use.) There is a real art to this counseling approach and if you practice and practice you will touch heart strings that no other agent will attempt. I also suggest you ask them to describe a perfect transaction. Sometimes they may need a little help understanding this question. Once they get it, they will say, "We want a full price offer with no turbulence, and we want to close in 30 days, and we don't want to make a double move." Take good notes and just keep asking for more. Your goal is to help them with their dreams. What is so lovely is if they say they want their home sold in 30 days then they just answered their own question of what price should they select...the 30-day price, the 60-day price or the 90 days or more price!

With this 5-6-7 interviewing formula, you now know what's important about buying or selling that touches their heart. This concept was originally developed through a book you should buy called *Values-Based Selling* by Bill Bachrach. It is absolutely a wonderful read around the art of building high-trust client relationships. The clients themselves learn and discover things about their purpose for moving that they themselves were not even aware of! Your average real estate agent or loan officer will never do this. This value-added method is also what makes you different. You are actually their consultant and advisor! It shows you care and are there to help them discover their needs and wants from the core of their heart! To best learn more about this as it relates to real estate, By Referral Only offers training around this concept. Go to www.MyByReferralonly.com or allow me to introduce you to a consultant who can help you understand this method by sending me an e-mail at Jim@HomeReferralTeam.net.

Chapter 10: *Favorite Referral List*

Also known as:
Team 100 or
Service directory

   Part of the key to your success as a real estate or lending consultant is surrounding yourself with the right people to help you get through the real estate transaction and even after the transaction closes. I strive to be the go-to guy for real estate and for all your professional needs that surround being a homeowner. I only refer people and businesses that have proven their work and charge a reasonable fee. At each of my consultations, I provide a hard copy of my latest list. Every year I spend about 20 hours updating this list as my team spends another 20 hours updating it as well. It's always such a masterpiece when we are done each year. Best of all, it provides service like no other to my friends and clients. It provides a service for life even if my clients never move again. It also creates a better yield on future introductions from my clients and friends in the future. Check it out at www.JimsJournal.net. Go to "Jim's Favorite Referrals" under categories. Take a minute to watch the video to understand more! I have always heard that you should "lead with the giving hand" and you will be taken care of for the rest of your life!

Chapter 11: *Why waiting to sell or buy could be the wrong choice*

There are many reasons and excuses to delay your move. You could say the market is bad or too good. You could say interest rates are too high and you want to wait until they drop. You also may think interest rates may drop, but in reality, nobody really knows and you may be missing out on a better home price now! The point is you need to take a good look at what's important about buying or selling to you. Your entire focus of timing should be around your deepest purpose for moving, <u>NOT</u> the current market or interest rates. In the grand scheme of things, most people down the road can't even remember what their interest rate is.

You say it is a bad market? How would you know if what you believe wasn't true? I am not going to say wait before you go for your deepest desire to move. Again, it all depends on where you live! Consult with a true real estate consultant and find out the facts. You may be surprised. Plus, focus on your 5-6-7, not things you can't control.

My clients are always surprised to hear how many homes have sold in their neighborhood in the last 12 months. Can you believe even in a slow market it can be a 7-10 percent turnover rate in your neighborhood? For example, in your 1,000 home communities, 100 homes have sold! This should be a part of every initial consultation to open the eyes of the seller and even the Realtor to show that yes there are other homes actually selling in our neighborhood.

Specifically what proof would you need to know that your belief that you can't sell right now is just not true and it is the right time for you to go for your deepest desire?

Do you find yourself speculating? Ask yourself that question. Have you checked out the facts?

Chapter 12: *The hard-to-sell properties*

I realize there are some disastrous properties out there, and you may be wondering how you could apply this formula to those types of homes. Remember: a home is worth what a buyer is willing to pay. There is a price for every home, which in turn means there is a buyer for every home.

One time I had a horrible home in an older up-and-coming neighborhood. This home needed everything! Even the walls didn't look structurally sound! I ran the similar home comparables in the area and we put it on the market at my 30-day price of $189,000. The offers started pouring in! One came in at $240,000 and the other one at $245,000, both cash offers! My seller was blown away! The two high bids were both investors and were going to scrap the home and rebuild. They saw more value in the land, and because we priced it at the sweet spot, we got more than even our 90-day price, and once again I was the hero! In this case, we absolutely created a buying frenzy, and because it was a hot area we saw wonderful results. This may be an extreme example in a hot little pocket at the time, but you can see good results in areas that are quite depressed too.

Chapter 13: *When your home still won't sell or when you can't find that home*

I don't have to tell you what to do when you get one or multiple offers. Let your real estate consultant negotiate on your behalf. Ask him what he would do. You might be surprised.

So what do you do when even a low price doesn't seem to be working? I won't lie to you and say that the 30-day price is a 100-percent cure-all sure thing. In rare cases, a home won't even sell at below market price. Recently I have heard of some extreme examples of banks pricing homes far below market price and even then they had trouble selling. There are many people who believe there is a deeper meaning when the home isn't selling, even on a spiritual level. I am a personal believer in this! God has a plan for everyone. I get close to my clients, and many times I can get a spiritual awareness that one party to the transaction is stopping the progress of the sale purely by their negative beliefs.

Two things I will say about this:

1. Let God guide you to that right 30-day price and whether selling now is the right time.
2. Pray daily for a home sale, and if your heart is truly in the right place, our maker Jesus Christ will bless you and answer your prayers.

You might be surprised that someone like me is talking about spiritual matters in a book like this. Let's face it – even if you as a real estate person are not a believer, you will come across clients who are. How are you going to handle this? Maybe you should get in touch with your spiritual side. It's important that you walk your talk. I personally can help you with this. Send me an e-mail: Jim@HomeReferralTeam.net and I will help you get in touch with your spiritual side. I would love to discuss your spiritual options as a home owner or a real estate consultant during a home sale and for your life.

Have you heard of those home sellers burying the Saint Joseph statue in the ground and then saying a daily prayer? Many people claim that this idea works. You can buy one of these statues at almost any Catholic store with instructions for home sellers. You can also Google Saint Joseph Statue and you can have one shipped to your home in a complete kit with instructions. Hey, don't knock this… many people have tried it even if they are not Catholic. My thought is at least it is getting people to pray, because the praying is what I believe makes the difference! There is power in prayer. You see, for those people in the family who are not ready, prayer sometimes helps get them ready and then I believe God helps things move forward and the home is sold! I'm sure you know that even some people who say they want to sell deep down are struggling with moving. It can be very emotional, and we as their consultants must be the strong and enduring light. A consultant must be a leader, and a good leader is a follower of Christ. A leader's instruction is in the good book! You as a homeowner need answers, and prayer can get you the answers and results you need. Make your relationship with God just that…a relationship.

Getting in touch with your spiritual side can do wonders for you as a leader! As a seller, you need to get in touch with your spiritual side because you may need to pray for purpose and desire. You may find that even after the sale that staying more in tune with the spirit will guide you through life with much more peace. Too many clients I work with, especially when they get somewhat older, tend to overthink things. Having faith and prayer will help you get through what seemed easier when you were younger and will get you through this change in your life.

I must not be remiss in the fact that home buyers need prayer in their home search as well as any home seller does. There is no "Saint Joseph" for home buyers to bury that I am aware of, but again the real meaning and purpose will come through the fact that seeking guidance from the Holy Spirit (sometimes referred to as the Holy Ghost) and from prayer will help guide you to your special home. You must pray not only for finding the right home but also for a home that will be a protection and a safe haven for possibly years to come. Just remember that you will never find 100 percent of what you are looking for. I will say that finding somewhere in the 90 percent range of what you are looking for is better than most home buyers find. So if you do find something that nice just feel blessed.

I am also a believer in a special prayer that should be said when you first move in your home that is sometimes referred to as a dedication prayer for your new home as you settle into your new abode. You certainly can attempt this prayer yourself, but if you don't feel comfortable, there are people you can find to help you. Here are a couple of suggestions if you decide to dedicate your own home: dedicate your home as a sanctuary for your family where family members can worship, find safety from the world, grow spiritually and prepare for family relationships that will continue for eternity.

Even before you pray for the right home, I suggest you pray for the right real estate consultant to help guide you to the right home. Think about how important his job is! You of course will be doing some searching on your home, but a hard working real estate consultant will find things you may not find!

I now hope you can catch the vision of how important spirituality is to your home selling and home buying process. I in fact have seen the sometimes unsettling times of this process uplifted to a higher level with the help of the powers above. Bringing spirituality into the mix can bring peace, joy and happiness into the process that will not be forgotten.

Chapter 14: *How this formula can successfully help home buyers too!*

When you are buying a home, whether it's your first one, an upgrade or an investment property, this formula – with the help of someone who really understands this concept – can greatly benefit you too! When you have selected a home to buy, don't get too anxious until you have researched the home and neighborhood to determine a 30-, 60- and 90+-day price. Regardless of what the home is listed for this information is valuable to you! As a buyer, you are looking to negotiate the best possible price – the 30-day price or less. As you negotiate, your real estate consultant can explain this concept to the other side and negotiate the right price for you as a buyer.

Too often the average real estate agent gets caught up in the excitement, sees the commission check and just writes up the contract without doing the proper research first. It doesn't take a skilled consultant long to determine the 30-day price! So take the time to find out before you write the contract. You will be glad you did, and you will be thanking me later after you do the research. It could save you thousands in the end! As a home buyer, you will love the fact that you bought the home knowing that you bought it at the 30-day price or better.

Chapter 15: *The magic words*

     I have to give 100 percent of the credit for this chapter to Joe Stumpf and his team at By Referral Only. By Referral Only helped me take this concept to a level I never could have dreamed of. Joe helped me relate the idea through dialogue known as Neuro-Linguistic Programming (NLP). It's a most powerful and persuasive form of communication. It's taking words we already know and putting them into the right order to accomplish magical results. It's like the combination to a safe. It puts the words we already use in the right order to open the safe! Of course, it's used to consult and advise your clients as if they were family members or close friends – in other words, it's not tricking them into doing something they shouldn't, it's a way to help people move forward towards what they want and then to do what's important to them. As their real estate consultant, you use this dialogue to bring them forward to their perfect goal you would honestly recommend. NLP is the most wonderful and amazing skill. To learn more about NLP, go to www.saladltd.co.uk, the web site of Salad Consulting in England. Founder Jamie Smart has developed a series of Irresistible Influence cards.

     If you are a Realtor or lender, you must go to www.ByReferralOnly.com and contact one of the coaches or business development consultant who will guide you through their secure website and an introduction to their magic word card decks. As a member of this community, they provide an entire dialogue coaching and training program I highly recommend. By Referral Only currently has four card decks of dialogues centered around real estate and lending that incorporate NLP. I believe this is cutting edge and absolutely the key to your success as a real estate consultant in today's marketplace. I have only been talking about one concept in this book I developed and am blessed they decided to use it. By Referral Only has dozens and dozens concepts and dialogue skills to lead you to success if you believe in and install the systems.

By Referral Only has taken my formula and developed language on how to present this to home sellers at the initial consultation. This language pattern can be found in their "Magic Words that Negotiate Agreements" black card deck. I'm going to give you this language pattern here in this book! (Refer to Chapter 9 to review the "5-6-7" concept before studying the Jack of spaces)

The focus is centered on what is important to the sellers by reminding them of the purpose of their move and how it stresses the beginning sales price! I can testify that your starting sales price makes all the difference in the world as to how the rest of the transaction occurs. I also love how the word "test" is used. It truly is a testing of sales price when you first put your home on the market. The card also emphasizes the three price options and how this reveals your sellers' true motivation level once you present their options based on time! It also shows whether they are 5-star clients.

If they don't choose the 30-day price, you still may choose to work with them because if they have to move, they will sell. You have given them the truth up front and if they didn't take your advice they won't blame you for the choices they made. It is completely magical and amazing!

Practice, practice, practice is what I suggest. Learn the script, but make it your own. It must not sound like a script. It must be conversational sounding language.

By the way, you can see how important it is for you to know their 5-6-7 before you actually can present this pricing formula. This way the focus is really about what is important to them and not the price. If you left out their dreams and desires, then you are just focusing on money and you will be less effective.

*Note: By Referral Only card decks and logos are copyrighted.

Here is the magic word dialogue for my 30/60/90-Day Pricing Formula that "By Referral Only" innovated on their jack of spades on page 41...

**Magic
Words
That
Negotiate
Agreements**

How To Use The 30/60/90-Day Pricing Formula

Have you found that the amount of time a person has to sell their home often determines what price they are willing to test?

Magic Words

I, like you, know how important your (5-6-7) is to you, but you may not know that how fast or slow you get (5-6-7) all depends on where you choose to begin to test your sales price. Based on what you told me (5-6-7), you have three choices to test. (1) A 30-day price of $_____. (2) A 60-day price of $_____. Or (3) a 90-days-or-more at $_____. What would happen if you test-priced it at $_____ because you really want (5-6-7)?

How To Use The
30/60/90-Day
Pricing Formula

Chapter 16: *Finding the consultant who believes in and has a passion for this formula*

Now that you have read this book, you want to find a real estate consultant who has this passion and understands this concept. You are welcome to contact one of my team members at 303-933-7000, log onto my team website or send us an e-mail at through our team website at: www.HomeReferralTeam.net. We will locate a By Referral Only consultant in your area who understands this concept. You can refer to the 30/60/90+-day pricing formula and/or the card deck . . . magic words that negotiate agreements. The exact card is the Jack of Spades. You see, my formula has become so popular with this community of over 5,000 real estate and lending consultants across our nation, I can locate someone to help you who knows this formula and can help you!

If you are a client of mine and have now read my book, I look forward to future success with your real estate endeavors!

--on your team
--with love
--and God bless you!

Jim Urban

P.S. I would love to hear your feedback now and in the future with your results and comments from reading this book. I prefer you log onto my Facebook account or blog and post a comment. Go to Facebook and type in "Jim Urban Denver" and you should find me, or go to www.JimsJournal.net.

Appendices

Most of the appendices can be found by logging onto
www.JimsJournal.net and clicking on the category 30/60/90
Home Pricing Formula, Foolproof Home Selling Strategies.
Scroll down to the bottom of the link and click on the
hyperlinks to access and modify the documents in Microsoft
Word.

Appendix A

30/60/90+ Day Home Pricing Formula and Net Estimate
Compliments of Jim A. Urban

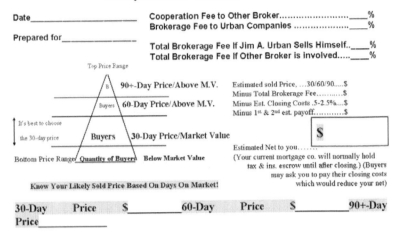

Date_____

Prepared for_____

Cooperation Fee to Other Broker..........................____%
Brokerage Fee to Urban Companies ....____%

Total Brokerage Fee If Jim A. Urban Sells Himself..____%
Total Brokerage Fee If Other Broker is involved.....____%

Top Price Range

B 90+-Day Price/Above M.V.

Buyers 60-Day Price/Above M.V.

It's best to choose
the 30-day price   Buyers   30-Day Price/Market Value

Bottom Price Range Quantity of Buyers Below Market Value

Estimated sold Price, ...30/60/90.....$
Minus Total Brokerage Fee...........$
Minus Est. Closing Costs .5-2.5%....$
Minus 1st & 2nd est. payoff............$

$ _____

Estimated Net to you........
(Your current mortgage co. will normally hold
tax & ins. escrow until after closing.) (Buyers
may ask you to pay their closing costs
which would reduce your net)

Know Your Likely Sold Price Based On Days On Market!

30-Day   Price $_____   60-Day   Price $_____   90+-Day   Price_____

Days on the market quoted may vary based on average price for your home. The more your home is above the average price for your area or town, the more likely you may have to consider a 60/90/120 (for a move-up home) or even a 90/120/150 (for a trophy home) days-on-the-market pricing strategy.

Important Money-Saving Points About Pricing Your Home Right (At the 30-Day Price):

- Should you select a real estate consultant based on price, or based on competence, trust and reputation?
- The best consultants are the ones who tell you the truth about the market value of your home up front.
- You should select your consultant first and then determine the market value of your home together.
- You should study not only the "for sale" homes in your area, but the "sold" and "under contract" homes as well. Your consultant should spend time with you reviewing these comparable homes.
- Your home should be priced normally at the top of the sold value and at the bottom of the for sale homes.
- The Comparative Market Analysis could include even the expired listings. Don't price your home near these prices or the same thing may happen to you (expire off the market, wasting your time and energy).
- Your value is primarily based on location. Other value factors include square footage and amenities, which include condition of the property (this being the least important of the three).
- Ask your consultant to strategize with you on price based on a rising market or a declining market so you don't get caught on the market too long or you leave money on the table at closing!
- A recent appraisal may not be a determination of your actual value. An appraisal for a refinance or insurance purposes may reflect a higher value, while an appraisal for a tax assessment or new mortgage may reflect a lower value. An accurate CMA provided by your real estate consultant will be your most accurate determination of actual value. The appraisal obtained by the buyer is critical, because if you did overprice the home, you may have to lower your price if the appraisal comes in lower – another reason to price your home right to begin with.
- Your home is worth what a buyer is willing to pay today, not what you paid for the home or what you hope the home may be worth. If you bought your home in a declining market, it could be worth less today.
- Ask your consultant which improvements you have made add value and which don't. Better yet, ask yourself if you had to do it over again right now knowing you are selling, would you still put the money into those improvements? Did you do those improvements for you, or did you do them with the intention of selling higher?
- The longer your home is on the market, the less negotiating power you have – another reason to price your home right from the beginning of your listing.
- Need for more money unfortunately doesn't adjust the market value of your home. The market does. You may have decided to stay and save the hassle of listing your home if you knew the truth up front from your consultant.
- Adding bargaining room is just another way to overprice your home.
- Pricing your home where it needs to be at the beginning doesn't mean you have to accept lower offers. You are in control. If you are priced right, sometimes you may even get multiple offers and it can create a showing frenzy. You may even sell higher than asking price! The more one person wants a home, the more others do!
- The peak interest of a listing is at the beginning, so trying it at a higher price will hinder your chances for a quick sale. Usually the largest number of showings occur within the first two weeks, due to a new home on the market that many buyers have not seen yet. Many buyers may not even know you are on the market because the top price range of their search doesn't extend into the price at which you listed your home.
- Buying up in a down market can actually benefit you as opposed to buying up in a rising market. (Ask me why.)
- Benefits of pricing your home right from the beginning are: **Faster sale, less inconvenience, more prospects, more agent enthusiasm, higher offers, higher net equity!**

Disclaimer:
This form is only an estimate based on what could happen and based on information provided to the Realtor by the Seller or Buyer and is not considered by any means the exact figures that will happen at an actual closing. This estimate is solely for the purpose of giving the customer and Realtor direction. Actual timing of the sale will vary and may sell earlier or later than the estimated time quoted based on initial list price. Market trends can change quickly and you must adjust your price accordingly

Appendix B

Fool-Proof Home-Selling Strategies!
30/60/90+ Home Pricing Strategy
Optional Home Staging
Optional Pre-Listing Home Inspection

Critical steps towards your ultimate scenario! The better the options you choose below, the sooner your dreams can be fulfilled! Remember, those dreams are _____

---

1) **Choose your best option after discussing the 30-day price, the 60-day price and the 90+-day price with your consultant.**
I select the 30-day price... Circle one: **Yes No** (Wholesale pricing, at or even below market value)
I select the 60-day price... Circle one: **Yes No** (Negotiating room, above market value)
I select the 90+-day price...Circle one: **Yes No** (Retail pricing, where most homes are priced)
(Note: if you choose number 2 and/or 3 below it is possible to affect the pricing strategy timing)

2) **Does my home need to be staged? Yes No I agree to have my home staged. Yes No**

(Note: Hiring a staging company to stage your home won't help if you are priced above market value.)
Having your home staged gives you an outside opinion of what should or could be done to the property to help attract more buyers to write a contract. Cost: $75 for initial consultation. (Cost may be more depending on size of home and services rendered.)

3) **Pre-Listing Home Inspection. I agree to have this completed. Yes No**

By having your home inspected prior to selling your home, it gives you a good idea what a buyer's inspection will report before you list your home. You can choose to fix and/or replace items that are discovered by the pre-listing inspector. The buyer reserves the right to hire their own inspector. Having this inspection completed and repairing possible issues now allows you to stay in control of the transaction. Cost $235.

I agree to participate in <u>all</u> of the Foolproof Selling Strategies and to do my best to follow all recommendations. I will allow my agent to contact their #2 and #3 references, and have them contact me for appointments as soon as possible. I understand that my minimum price for #2 and #3 combined will be $310 and is subject to increase depending on the size of my home and services rendered.

X_____date___ X_____date____

I agree to part of the Foolproof Selling Strategies.
I agree to (circle one) #2 #3 None (I just want to price my home to sell, and sell it AS-IS and use price as a "cure-all") Cost $_____. I agree to allow my agent to contact the #2 or #3 reference and have them contact me for appointments as soon as possible.

X_____date___ X_____date____

Disclaimer:
Choosing options on this document can increase the chances of selling but are in no way a guarantee of selling for any price and/or any time frame. After implementing all options above and if the home still does not sell could indicate that the market value has continued to decline and/or the home is beyond marketability and salability at this time.

Appendix C

30/60/90+ Day Home Pricing Strategy

30-Day Price

• This is your market value or below market value price

• 75% of all "Multiple Listing Service for sale homes" are above the market value as determined by the sold comparable homes.

• To sell faster, you must compete with a better, more competitive price.

• Market value is based primarily on location, square footage and condition.

• The terms and your real estate consultant are also factors in the marketability of your home.

• Price can be a "cure-all" for the problems a home may have. In other words, a lower price can cure other problems. Every home has a price break that will break open the market with buyers!

60-Day Price

• This is your slightly above market value price.

• Even just adding negotiating room can trigger a longer time to sell.

• The market will always adjust to your home's true value.

• Get the true market value up front from a consultant who truly investigates the market so you understand where you need to be.

• The only way you can get higher than market value in price is by offering bonuses or perks. For example: you offer to pay the buyers closing costs, a carpet or decorating allowance or "owner will carry" terms; or you are more flexible on the timing than the buyer is.

90+-Day Price

• This price is pushing others to think:

-They are just too high!

-What were they thinking?

-Did their realtor suggest this price?

• Often choosing this price will require you to adjust your price lower throughout the listing process for 90 or many more days!

• You most likely will sell your home for even lower than market value by starting too high. This price is not recommended.

• When you are on the market for 90+ days, you automatically become a "stale" listing. This gives you a disadvantage when you finally are able to negotiate your best price

51

Appendix D

What is important about_____to you?

What do you really, really, really want?

| 7 |

How would it feel for you to_____?

| 6 |

I'm wondering what would happen if you didn't get_____?

| 5 |

| 4 |

What happens when you imagine that? Or having that?

| 3 |

What's driving that choice right now?

| 2 |

Specifically, can you tell me more about that?

| 1 |

Additional questions:

1) Describe to me a perfect sale... _____ Anything else?

_____Anything else? _____

2) What is a perfect real estate consultant to you?_____

3) Who is the next person you know right now that will be (selling a home like you?) or (buying a home like you?)

_____

2) I'm curious what option you have decided on... will it be 1, 2, 3 or me?

4) I am your go-to guy! I want to recommend you include my cell phone number in your cell phone directory. This is great for any help you may need, or questions or referrals you may have. Can you program that now?

About the author

Jim A. Urban has held his Colorado Real Estate License and worked in the field since 1984. He is a Certified Residential Specialist (CRS) and alumni member of By Referral Only. Jim attended the University of Northern Colorado and majored in Business Administration.

Married since 1982, Jim and his wife Susan have four daughters: Bethany, 24; Elissa, 22; Kendra, 19; and Janelle, 16. Their oldest, Bethany, is married to Casey Jackman.

Jim's interests include bicycling, family, vacations, travel, and leading and inspiring others. Bicycling is a great passion of his. He participates at least three times a year in organized road cycling rides like Bicycle Tour of Colorado, Ride The Rockies, The Triple By Pass and various charity rides.

Reading business and self-help books is a hobby of Jim's. He is part of a weekly book readers club that reads and discusses at least two to three books a year. The club has had success inviting authors to visit. Jim also hosts a monthly Mastermind group with like-minded professionals in the Denver area.

Jim loves to blog (www.JimsJournal.net). He posts at least twice a week and works at finding ways to help clients, family, friends, neighbors, co-workers and peers in the real estate business. He enjoys inventing new and better ways to make humans have a better life on this planet. He also is very involved in his church, the Church of Jesus Christ of Latter Day Saints, and has a passion to help and serve people. Jim's second daughter is currently serving a mission for the church in Buenos Aires, Argentina.

Made in the USA
Lexington, KY
08 October 2013